discovermore

Life in a Community

Community Services

Dwayne Hicks

Britannica
Educational Publishing

IN ASSOCIATION WITH

THE ROSEN PUBLISHING GROUP

Published in 2024 by Britannica Educational Publishing (a trademark of Encyclopædia Britannica, Inc.) in association with The Rosen Publishing Group, Inc.
2544 Clinton Street, Buffalo, NY 14224

Distributed exclusively by Rosen Publishing.
To see additional Britannica Educational Publishing titles, go to rosenpublishing.com.

Editor: Greg Roza
Book Design: Leslie Taylor

Photo Credits: Cover Motortion Films/Shutterstock.com; (series background) Dai Yim/Shutterstock.com; p. 5 (top) Avatar_023/Shutterstock.com; p. 5 (bottom) FamVeld/Shutterstock.com; p. 6 PR Image Factory/Shutterstock.com; p. 7 Roman Zaiets/Shutterstock.com; p. 8 Tyler Olson/Shutterstock.com; p. 9 shisu_ka/Shutterstock.com; p. 10 leungchopan/Shutterstock.com; p. 11 Bob Pool/Shutterstock.com; p. 12 Eric Isselee/Shutterstock.com; p. 13 Pamela Brick/Shutterstock.com; p. 14 Kzenon/Shutterstock.com; p. 15 Christian Schwier/Shutterstock.com; p. 16 Air Images/Shutterstock.com; p. 17 Gorodenkoff/Shutterstock.com; p. 19 (top) William Perugini/Shutterstock.com; p. 19 (bottom) GaudiLab/Shutterstock.com; p. 20 Sean Locke Photography/Shutterstock.com; p. 21 Girts Ragelis/Shutterstock.com; p. 23 (top) Ihi/Shutterstock.com; p. 23 (bottom) Jonathan Weiss/Shutterstock.com; p. 24 Trong Nguyen/Shutterstock.com; p. 25 wavebreakmedia/Shutterstock.com; p. 26 Kenneth Sponsler/Shutterstock.com; p. 27 joyfull/Shutterstock.com; p. 28 LanaG/Shutterstock.com; p. 29 BearFotos/Shutterstock.com.

Library of Congress Cataloging-in-Publication Data

Names: Hicks, Dwayne.
Title: Community services / Dwayne Hicks.
Description: New York : Britannica Educational Publishing, in Association with Rosen Educational Services. 2024. | Series: Discover more: life in a community | Includes glossary and index.
Identifiers: ISBN 9781642828818 (library bound) | ISBN 9781642828801 (pbk) | ISBN 9781642828825 (ebook)
Subjects: LCSH: Community life--Juvenile literature. | Community organization--Juvenile literature. | Municipal services--Juvenile literature.
Classification: LCC HM761.H53 2024 | DDC 307–dc23

Manufactured in the United States of America

Some of the images in this book illustrate individuals who are models. The depictions do not imply actual situations or events.

CPSIA Compliance Information: Batch #CSBRIT24. For further information contact Rosen Publishing at 1-800-237-9932.

Contents

Serving the Community

A group of people who live in the same place and share the same resources is called a community. A community, whether large or small, also provides services to meet the needs and wants of its members.

Needs are what people must have in order to survive: a place to live, food to eat, and water to drink. Wants are things that people would like to have but that are not necessary for survival, such as a new bike or car. Goods and services satisfy people's wants and needs.

Goods include such objects as apples, cars, and roads. Services are things that people do for others. Gymnastics lessons, banking, and dental care are all services.

Take a walk, pedal a bike, or ride in a car to explore a nearby community. How many different community services can you find?

Clean, safe water to drink is a need.

compare and contrast

Grocery stores provide both wants and needs. Look in your shopping cart. Which items are needs and which are wants? Now ask a parent if they agree.

A fun swimming pool is a want.

What's Your Community Like?

There are many different kinds of communities. Urban communities are large cities with many people, buildings, and businesses. Areas called suburbs lie outside the boundaries of cities. Many people live in the suburbs and commute, or travel, to their jobs in the city. Rural communities are small and out in the country away from cities or suburbs.

Taking public transportation costs less than owning a car. This means people can easily travel to their jobs, even if they don't make a lot of money.

Public transportation makes it possible for people with disabilities to get where they need to go.

Communities have two kinds of services available to their citizens: private and public. Private services are those that individuals provide. People pay money directly to businesses for private services, such as a stylist cutting hair or a veterinarian caring for a sick pet. Public services are provided by the community. The members of the community pay for the services through taxes, or money that the members pay to the community. Public services are things that make the community better and safer for everyone who lives there.

Consider This

What happens when there's an emergency in your community? Does your community have its own emergency services? Or do people need to wait for workers and equipment from the next larger community?

Safety and Security

Keeping people and property safe is important in any community. People trust that their police, fire, and ambulance services are ready to help if there's an accident or crime. Families feel secure because of community safety services.

People who work earn an income. Workers deposit their money in bank accounts at banks and credit unions. Most people have a checking account, so they can write checks to pay for goods and services for their family.

Most communities have fire departments. Firefighters train to be able to protect people in an emergency.

Banks provide valuable services to the people who live in communities. They help protect the money that people work hard for.

Some people also keep money in savings accounts to earn interest. Interest is money that the bank pays for every dollar that someone has in their savings account.

Some people borrow money from banks. Loans help them buy expensive items like homes or cars. People pay the loan back in monthly portions called installments. If the loan is for a big purchase, such as a car or house, the item is **collateral** against repayment of the loan.

WORD WISE

Collateral is something that a bank can take back if someone fails to repay a loan.

So Much to Discover!

School isn't the only place people go to learn new things. Community members of all ages can learn about math, mice, moths, and more at libraries and museums. Teachers, librarians, and museum curators work to educate others at these institutions.

Students on a field trip visit interesting places in their community. There's a lot you can learn outside a classroom!

Consider This

Did you know that libraries are connected by technology? If you need a book that your local library doesn't own, the librarian might be able to borrow it from another library—even one that's far away. This is called an interlibrary loan.

Interpreters at living history museums demonstrate what life was like long ago.

Schools are places where children go to learn. Every school serves the same purpose: to educate students.

A library has books, newspapers, magazines, films, audio recordings, and computer software. Most public libraries have computers that people can use for free. Librarians keep the resources in order. They show people how to find and use them.

Museums inspire interest and understanding by displaying objects from many different times and places. They may also offer services such as guided tours, lectures, and special events. Scientists and other scholars sometimes use museums to do research. Many museums have apps you can use to learn more about the items on display.

Keeping Everyone Healthy

Any member of a community can get hurt or sick. People sprain their ankles, catch colds, and get toothaches. Their pets get fleas and hurt their paws. In a community, citizens have places to go to receive medical care.

People want to be healthy, so they count on others to provide medical services. Someone with a serious injury goes to the hospital **emergency room** for treatment.

Veterinarians take care of all the animals in a community. In a rural area, this might include horses, cows, and pigs too!

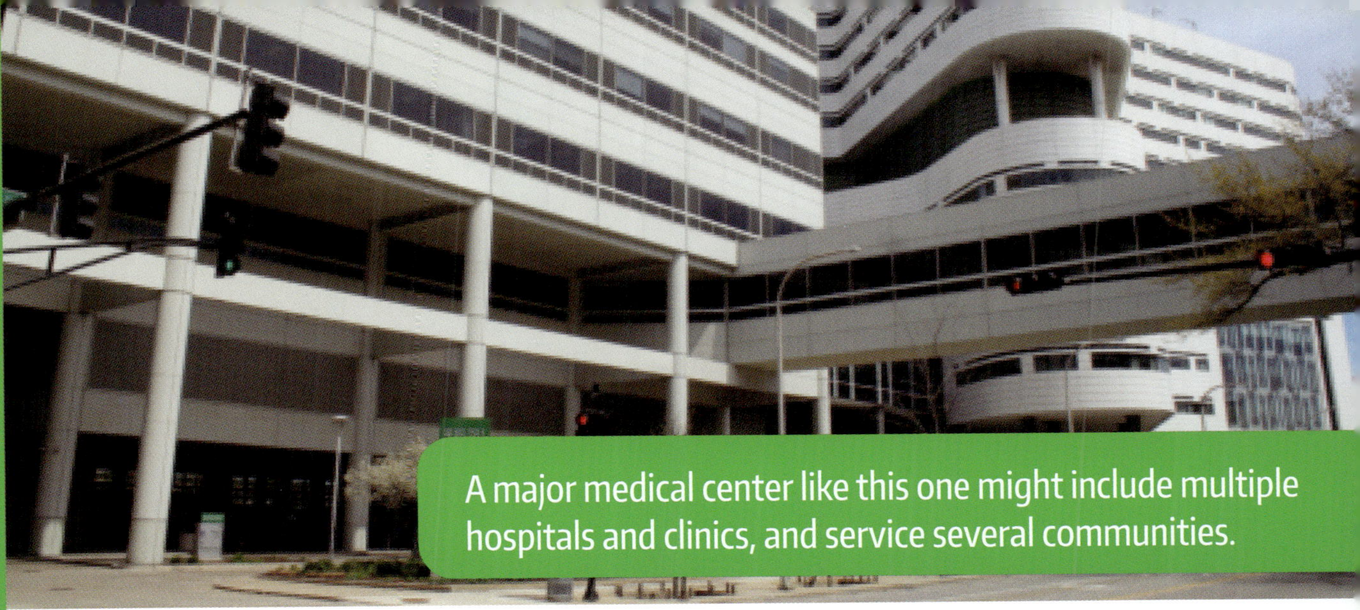

A major medical center like this one might include multiple hospitals and clinics, and service several communities.

Parents take sick children to see the doctor at an office or clinic. Someone with a sore tooth makes a dental appointment. Pet owners hurry their wounded dog to the veterinarian.

Doctors are people with many years of education and training. They are skilled specialists who help keep people healthy and heal the sick. Dentists, nurses, veterinarians, and other health care workers are also highly skilled. Health care workers are vitally important to all communities.

WORD WISE

An emergency room (ER) is the department of a hospital that treats people in need of immediate care.

Keeping Things Clean

Everyone wants their community to be a clean and healthy place to live. Recycling centers, garbage pick-up, and water treatment plants help keep communities clean and also protect their natural resources.

Many materials—aluminum cans, glass bottles, newspapers, magazines, and plastics—can be recycled. Recycling reuses materials instead of throwing them away to pollute the land, air, and water. In some communities, recycling and garbage pick-up are private services. In others, the services are provided by the community. Members of the community receive the services because they pay taxes to the community.

A compost plant recycles organic waste such as food scraps and manure into rich healthy soil.

A reservoir is a large lake, usually human-made, where a community's water supply is stored.

In some areas, people get their water straight from a river or a well. Large cities and towns, however, have public systems that provide water to their residents and businesses. Municipal water companies filter and distribute clean water. Generally, people pay a fee for the water their household **consumes** and for using the community's sewer system.

WORD WISE

To consume something is to use it. People consume water when they drink it, but also when they use it to wash things or to fill swimming pools.

Roads, Roofs, and Repairs

Communities are always growing and changing. They need to construct new buildings for people to live and work in. They also need to build and repair freeways, roads, and bridges. These structures help keep communities operating. Construction workers perform all of this work. Many different kinds of workers may be involved in a construction project. Some have particular skills. Electricians, plumbers, roofers, and carpenters are all special types of workers.

Someone who wants to be a plumber, electrician, or mason might study at a trade school, instead of a college.

There are many steps involved in designing a new building. Where will people park their cars? Can the community provide enough electricity?

Construction workers may be hired by a city to work on public projects or they may be hired by individuals. For example, potholes make the streets bumpy and difficult to drive on. City workers fill and fix potholes to make the road smooth again. Your parents might hire a private contractor to install a new driveway at your house.

Consider This

Are there any buildings under construction in your community right now? How many kinds of workers do you think are involved?

All Around the Town

There are many different ways to move from place to place within your community. You can walk to school or the playground, bicycle to the park, drive a car to work, or ride a bus to the mall. People also use transportation to move goods from one place to another. When crops are ready, farmers box and send them to market. Sometimes, this is a small, local market where people from the area come to buy fresh food. Other times, the food is loaded onto large trucks and shipped to supermarkets far away.

Communities usually offer plenty of transportation services. Citizens fill their gas tanks at gas stations and have their vehicles repaired at service stations. Bicycle shops sell and repair bikes. If you want to travel to a different community, you might take a plane or train.

There are different kinds of train service. People might take a subway to get to work or school within their own community.

compare and contrast

In many communities, kids ride a school bus to school every day. Suppose there was no school bus. How many other ways could you get to and from school?

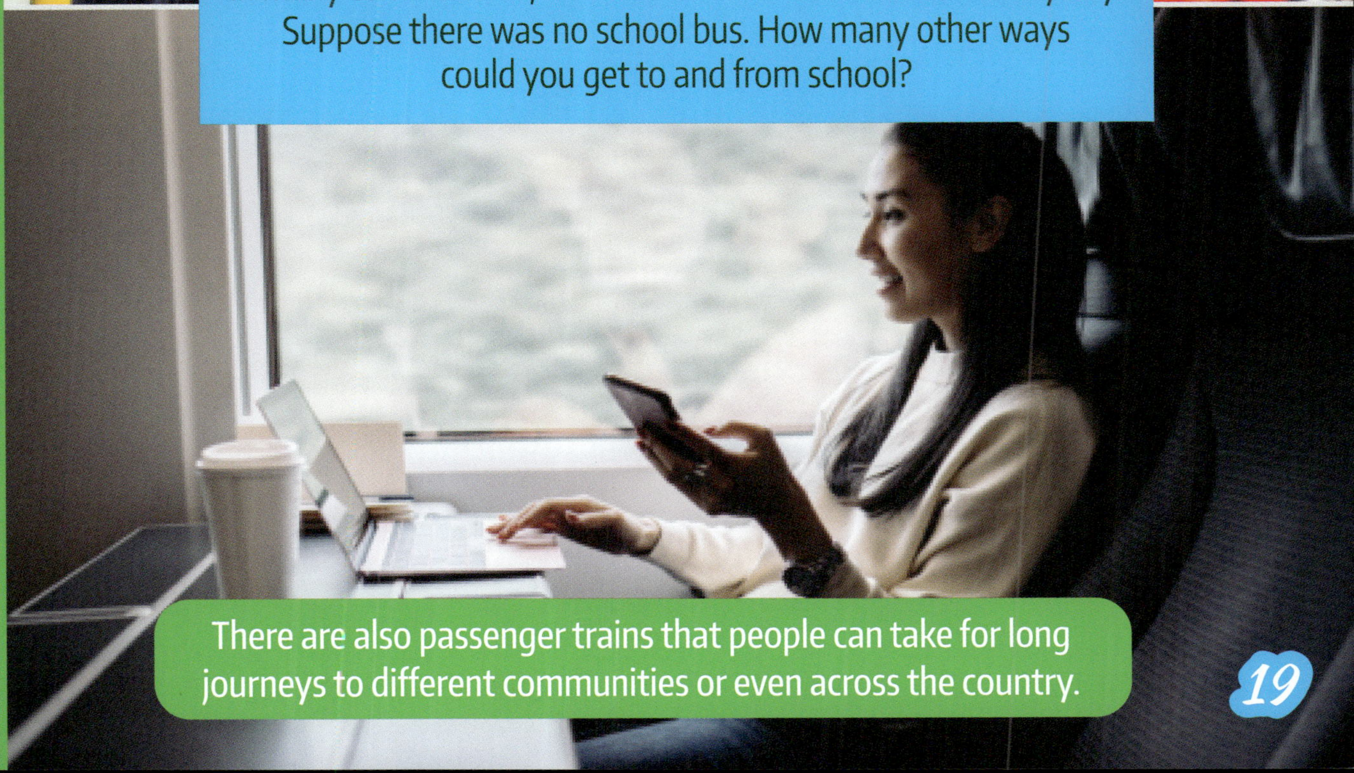

There are also passenger trains that people can take for long journeys to different communities or even across the country.

You've Got Mail

How many ways can you think of to communicate with others? All day long, people send and receive messages. Communication can be fun, like getting a birthday present in the mail. Communication can be important, like telling a parent what time soccer practice is over. And communication can be alarming, like calling 911 for someone who has been in an accident or is hurt.

It's fun to receive packages in the mail.

Video calls via internet help people conduct business with offices that are far away.

Many community businesses and services help people communicate. At the post office, people mail letters and packages. Mail can be sent almost anywhere in the world. The telecommunications industry allows citizens to communicate in different ways. Most people used to have traditional telephones in their homes. Now almost everyone carries a cell phone or smartphone to stay in touch wherever they go. They can access the internet on their phone or on their computer.

Consider This

How did your family use communications services during the COVID-19 pandemic? Did you go to school or talk to relatives on video calls? Did you do your shopping via the internet?

What's for Dinner?

There are many different ways people get food to eat. In rural communities, people often live on farms and grow their own food. In cities, people shop for food at grocery stores, supermarkets, and local farmers' markets. City dwellers may also choose to eat out at restaurants. They may have a favorite restaurant in their community.

The farmers that grow crops and raise animals are providing a service. When food or crops are ready, farmers ship them to markets and to restaurants. If the market is nearby, a farmer's products arrive by truck. If the market is far away, products are transported by truck, train, or ship. People who cook and serve food in restaurants, schools, or hospitals also provide a valuable community service.

In some communities, the main industry is catching fish or other kinds of marine life that people like to eat.

compareandcontrast

Where does your family usually buy food? A big supermarket? A tiny neighborhood bodega? Or do you order it online and have it delivered?

People can't concentrate on school or work if they're hungry. Many communities have programs to help people buy food if they're out of work or sick.

Just for Fun

There's more to a community than just work and school. Many communities have fun recreational facilities. Some people enjoy the outdoors. They hike the trails at a neighborhood park or swim and splash in the pool. Some climb and swing at the playground. They slide down snowy hills or skate across smooth ice. Many parks also sell tasty treats.

Some community parks have fun water fountains for cooling off on hot summer days.

An indoor climbing wall is a great way to practice if the weather's too harsh to be outside.

Other people might prefer indoor fun. They can watch a movie at the theater or play electronic games at a video arcade. Some like to roll a strike at the bowling alley or shoot baskets at an indoor gym or community center.

Community members can choose what they do for fun. Most communities try to offer a variety of fun activities for residents.

Consider This

Where does your family go to have fun? Are there facilities where you live, or do you have to visit another community?

Picture Perfect!

People like to look nice when they go out. They do this by getting their hair styled or by wearing nice clothes. There are many different kinds of stores that help people look good.

Hair salons, barbershops, clothing stores, shoe stores, and eyeglass stores are found in many communities. Larger communities have many stores. They have huge shopping malls where consumers purchase many different kinds of goods and services in one place. Smaller communities usually have fewer stores to provide the citizens' needs and wants.

A small town may have family-owned shops like a barber or tailor. Doing business with them keeps money right in your community.

A large shopping mall has many more choices for clothing, accessories, and beauty services. However, mall stores are generally owned by large **corporations** instead of your neighbors.

In communities where several stores sell the same goods or provide the same services, producers must compete for customers. Competition is good for businesses and consumers. Businesses must offer great prices and service, and customers get to pick the very best deals.

WORD WISE

A corporation is a large business or organization.

Changing with the Times

Life is always changing, even in the smallest communities. Years ago, people rode horses and used them for farm work. Stagecoaches transported people and goods using horses. The wide use of horses meant that there used to be special workers and services for horses and the people who used them. For example, blacksmiths made and repaired equipment used for horses and horse travel. Today, people still ride horses, but the services to support them are not as necessary.

In most American communities today, horseback riding has changed from a need to a want. People have other ways to get around, but they ride horses for fun.

Libraries often have important community records and documents in their collections. They also offer classes in the latest computer programs, all in the same place. How amazing is that?

Other services have changed as well. Public libraries, for instance, offer more services than just borrowing books. Libraries now provide computer and tablet rentals, online resources, and help for people seeking jobs.

Community services are available wherever people live, work, and play. From the horses of yesterday to the electric cars of today—and beyond—community services will continue to grow to suit citizens' needs.

Consider This

Electric cars are becoming more common in many places. What sort of community services do you think will be needed for them?

Glossary

compete: To strive for something.

consumer: A person who buys and uses goods and services.

deposit: To put money in a bank.

goods: Manufactured articles or products of art or craft.

industry: The businesses that provide a particular product or service.

loan: Money lent at interest.

market: A meeting together of people to buy and sell.

pollute: To spoil (as a natural resource) with waste made by humans.

producer: A person who grows agricultural products or manufactures articles.

recreational: Done for enjoyment.

recycling: Reusing materials instead of throwing them away.

rural: Of or relating to the country, country people or life, or agriculture.

services: Useful labor that does not produce goods.

supermarket: A market selling foods and household items.

telecommunications: Communication that takes place across a distance.

transportation: Method of moving from one place to another.

urban: Related to or typical of being in a city.

For More Information

Books

Evans, Shira. *National Geographic Readers: Helpers in Your Neighborhood*. Washington, D.C.: National Geographic Kids, 2018.

Ventura, Marne. *Goods and Services*. Minneapolis, MN: Cody Koala, 2018.

Websites

At-home Activities for Kids

www.pbs.org/parents/community-helpers

PBS Kids has a selection of crafts and activities about the people who provides services in communities.

Games About Community Helpers

thekindergartenconnection.com/community-helpers-bingo/

The Kindergarten Connection has a printable bingo game about community helpers and links to more fun activities.

Index